Love in the Time of Corona:

Notes from a Pandemic

Edited by
Lynnette Lounsbury & Charlotte O'Neill
2020

First printing October 2020

ISBN: 9798697675281

This book is dedicated to

Carolyn Rickett
a long-time champion
of creative writing at Avondale

In early 2020 we started to hear rumours about a virus out of Wuhan, China. They were vague and distant and we engaged only on the superficial level of curiosity. We were far too busy trying to put out the six-month bushfire that ravaged Australia. And then the floods.

By March 23 we were in shutdown – students who had signed up for a workshop based, interactive creative writing class were stuck with Zoom lectures that were fraught with interruptions and glitches, and which survived on the whim of an over-crowded NBN.

The rules of the shutdown meant that we could only leave our homes to buy food, for medical care or to exercise. Fines were in place for those who broke the rules. Everyone broke a few of them. The phrase "unprecedented times" became our nemesis. The days were long and empty; identical to the point of confusion. We moved from bored and listless to motivated and over-stimulated within hours. At the time of writing this, we were in the second wave of lockdowns.

And yet – we wrote poetry. And we wrote stories. And

we shared what we loved across our screens and we
pushed ourselves to find words to describe what was
happening, what we were thinking and dreaming about,
and we tried to inspire and entertain each other. Poetry
is universal. Stories are timeless. We created something

from a time that felt formless. We were made expansive
as we wrote. Some of our work was simple, rudimentary,
rhythmless and rambling. But much of it is beautiful,
passionate, truthful and even genius. It is our humanity
in this small moment and it is our remembrance and our
celebration of a time without... what is the word I'm
looking for... a time... without precedence.

-    Lynnette Lounsbury

POETRY

Amity Bradford

the transaction

she willed the
misshapen
moon to rise

and shook hands
with fog
as she passed.

payment,
finally, in the form
of breath

trudging through blackness
loaded hearts
and light hands.

fading altogether in the
startling evening dawn.

a full shoerack

i haven't worn
shoes in weeks

my slippers and bedsocks
don't count.

they are all that
i wear as

my centipede
days are over

now i legally
can't leave my house.

so, which
is more important here:

souls or soles?

Ashley Cotter

a different horizon

the slip on quiet
ease
blanket over morning
over face

a dip in coolness
sea salt swells
the heart
not quite

a gentle bite
fierce peaks release
air that strangles
silent escape

forever horizon
interrupted sky
in the fringe of shadows
lies joy

chorreador

the chorreador brings
memories arousing
in san francisco

lazy sunday mornings
the streets sleeping
under a cool fog blanket

quiet laughs and
silent steaming
from our mugs

black grounds in the
sink speckling
each other in warmth

the chorreador sits
in its worn wooden framing
our faces

loud tears and
screams from the people that
wander down below echoing
cold coffee

the chorreador rests
still in the absence from
the front door left widening
space in shadowed rooms

ceramic shards nestling
cotton cloth on
wood floors

Caitlin Jankiewitz

#SocialDistancing

Hands extend
      through anxious pixels
         Blue touch
faces glowing   with late night
     news insisting
On being read
     Ringing   heavy
silence hanging
Between us   radio static
     meandering through the lost
Forgotten mental tunnels
     Of an unchained melody
Slowly
     slipping
       grains of sanity
Young love   sputters
     In the twilight shroud
Of one point five
     meters of cyber glass

The Bee

They told me I was fortunate
That the gods of genetics
Had smiled on me as womanhood
Began to blossom in my soft places
They said I'd be the envy
Of many who longed for that same
thick sweet femininity flowing
heavy in my veins
Blooming on my underwear
As my body swelled
With pride at its natural being
I wore it with innocence
Oblivious and ignorant
To the secret stares and ravenous thoughts
That lay behind dull and adoring eyes
You were the first
To unearth my form, to trace
My lines and curves with a vagrant finger
Droning your approval
Encircling that which you assumed yours
Scratching dregs of neckline dignity
As you drank of my nectar
You pried loose my body, ignoring
The rending cries of my mind
Chiseling out the pieces you liked best
To be kept with other shiny objects
In a dresser drawer
My duty, you hummed, my fault
For inhabiting this shape
As if I would choose
To have you trample my petals
And make me believe
That being bruised is normal
Because after all
Flowers die waiting
For the bee

Calum Entermann

amen

fists shaken at skies
deep breaths drawn out at sunsets
both may be prayer

melody

You mean
more than
I should have
let you,
this is why
we must
fort-knox
our hearts,
I'll leave you
there
a while longer,   suspended
in silence
rather
you think me
indifferent
than have you
know
you are my
song.

honest

bottle honesty's sound
next time it graces you
with it's clear-glass cup

the word
looks like
'honey'
honesty
'honey'
and sounds
candy sweet

the action
like honey
down
your chin
sticky hair
and ants,
black ants
everywhere

sounds like
loud voices,
lump in the throat
discarded smiles
lost eye contact

and
Daddy's not coming,
Pills in my draw,
Mom I'm pregnant,
and
Dad I'm gay
It wasn't your best,
I crashed the car,
and
Please don't call,
I feel lonely,
You hurt me,

harness honesty's sound
next time it graces you
with a left hook,
invites you sit in its
un-padded seats,
clear-glass slit
your hand

bottle all the noise
that is,
if you can endure
nails drawn down
chalkboards
or see through
those cloud tears

Kathryn Staples

isolation

The sun now taunts me
Its fingers begging for company.
Clear windows morphing
into bars.
The outside now an addiction.
Craving, to step over
the threshold.
Looking over your shoulder,
making sure the green zone
is unbroken.
Invisible walls expanding
keeping out intruders.
Fear, creeping around the corner.
This is war.
The new norm.

this is me

A fortress of protection.
Once comforting
now a prison, trapping
my soul.
The pounding drums
I can't concentrate.
Dreams melting through my fingers.
        Self, fading away.
My protectors vision
a flame.
Piercing voices fill the void.
My friends whisper a tornado,
        who am I?
 Am I the woman parents want?
Am I the woman friends envisage?
Am I the woman I see I am?
        I am all, I am neither.
One trip away.
Away from piercing voices,
Away from whispers.
Fantasy now reality
engulfing, spreading like fire.
Cleansing my soul.
New growth full of bright colours
warm and comforting.
   This is me.
            This is who I am.

Lachlan Bilson

the beast

tendrils tangle round my mind
I find I'm gasping intertwined
the world can seem to fall behind
as time suffocates time

memories from my mother's prime
claw mark chest scars ill-defined
accomplices with pockets lined
and time suffocates time

my brother's body we couldn't find
teeth torn arms too well confined
if only one of us wasn't blind
still time suffocates time

our children though they tried to hide
caught by the beast and truly I'd
like to think they'll make it,
but time suffocates time.

supper time

I focus on the impermanence,
how every joy will falter,
how every laugh will fade,
how in each great performance a finale must be staged.
How leaves wilt in winter
as the weary waste away,
how the playgrounds have rusted
where the children used to play.
I think of my now hole-filled jeans,
oil stained in the rag bin.
Could have beens, would have beens
have beens and has beens.
The darkness after sunset,
the drought after dew
I think of the many,
though they're now just a few.
I remember how a breeze can come
to awaken stale airs,
how every grand finale
needs a man to stack the chairs.
How green leaves grow back,
and over graves new children play.
I chuckle thinking of the jeans
I picked up the other day.
Tears dry, cries fall to sighs,
drought breaks away to rains.
I find a way to stand again
although nothing remains.
For impermanence strikes a second stroke,
And I've learned not to be bitter,
because there's every chance, any chance
things could be better after dinner.

Lauren McMahon

isolation

Mindlessness existence
Sinking head to couch
All day to eat breakfast
            huff
Time never runs out

Solitary confinement
White imaginary walls
Running on low battery
            huff
Scrubbing off the war

Army of pyjamas
Statistic is my name
Delivery man my only friend
            huff
Is this all a con game?

Front door glued shut
Weeks amalgamated
Sanitised social media
            huff
Isolation; a pandemic

confessions of a daydreamer

Tourist in the waking world
Never quite awake
Stuck in a subconscious story
What is real? What is fake?

Exotic lands and whimsical beings
I am the artist of a new cosmos
Eyes open, heart pumping
Imagination overdose

Triumphant adventures
Frolicking in sun showers
You may think I'm crazy
Unless you too, are a daydreamer

Sally-Mae Herford

#isolation

A day, friend of new
deliciously dangerous
of golden eyes, honeyed hair
eyes of deceit and naivety

Most days, spent within childish laughter
for the most part, it's nice
not wonderful, nice

One day, golden eyes turn darkened
where laughter resided, now joylessness
mockery takes up her cruel vacancy

That day, hurt turned routine
your eyes grew sunken
and your waist forgets the food
you leave

The days, following, become anew
growth makes way for adolescents
her darkness seems as a distant remembrance

Some days, you see her
at the post office, in the street, at the store with her
mum
but you aren't bitter

These days, you're different
where once cracks and dark places
now days of contentedness

Then one day, the past snatches you back
the past now tainted present

Your days, spent in delight
her days, suffocated in sorrow
and in one day, she decided to leave

And you realise that you are lucky
to have all the days
she left behind
even if it is one day

c o n f e s s i o n a l

When was I promised immunity?
When I grew rounder and life began to sting?
That oh-so-lovely sting
        I can't recall anymore

The whispers at the end of the hall are growing louder
now
To translate would be a worthless plight
        I dread my silence to be taken as fact
Why bother them?

Where can I go now?
'To the morgue with her'
Pounds upon pounds of rotted flesh
A silence I brought upon myself
        I am to blame
Where can I run now?

Too stubborn to ask for help
"Have you no understanding for this hollowed heart?" I
lament
        I suppose to the grave I must go
All fancified and false

Upon the moulded concrete it read's
'Here lies squandered youth'
oh, what a bleak swan song
        I will remain there, silent
for I am not yet twenty-four

Linda Edorsson

not in the same boat

Hard to port
A storm is bursting canvas out at sea
I see Catamarans and Dinghies manoeuvring waves
Galleons, Yachts, and Pontoons drifting into the
unknown

Tales of sea monsters reach our shores
We make notes on our maps
Terra incognita, stay clear of the edge
Ferries, Gondolas, and Tankers return
Jukungs, Navals, and Trawlers head out
Punting is lost, so is the Bowrider
Floating houses like a pearl necklace on the horizon

evenly spread apart

A Canoe and a Kayak paddle quietly side by side
A Shooner is shipwrecked, a Bateau capsized
A Barge heads upstream
    We scorn the Cruise Ships but we are all just boats
               floating in the same ocean
   Connected on the surface but divided by the depths
Riding out the storm
They say we're in this together
but you're a Brig and I am a Sloop

there is more

I wear my armour for protection but underneath I tear
flesh open to air and fester   I turn wine into water and
drink while I wait and whisper to my heart   stay
frozen   my ribcage carries a cumulonimbus
cloud   towering up my throat   I keep my skin thick
bones hollow   my mind screaming into a pillow
God is silent   Raise me all over again and I'll
squirm spit and strike   like a cobra
don't tread on my head   I'm not a child or
dead   I'm fine   I wait for signs and miracles
they do not grace me with their presence   They are
fading memories in a rear-view mirage   A fragile
mirror   there has to be more   What does
it all mean to be saved or sain   both or neither
I used to have wings   unstoppable
never resting   always homesick for other worlds   for
deeper roots but   I'm fine   I
stay silent   I go without direction
I make my own   my own   clouds are
gathering
there has to be more
Where do I end and God begin   When does God begin
when I end   When I stop   God how do I stop
Raise me from the dead or worse   like a child   I am
neither   I am fine
I am heart-strong with a head patched by a thousand
pieces   I run   trying to keep up   grasping at
moments   looking down alleys and around corners
I test   I try   I think a lot
Thunder   rage   and madness chiselled these words on
my walls   there is more
My hero and nightmare held a sliver of truth

There is more

I'm fine
There is peace in nimbus   I watch it roar through my
kaleidoscope and I mend shattered pieces into
wholeness
I don't know
but   there is more

Lynnette Lounsbury

it is the dream

it is the dream
        the silence bubbling gently on the stove,
        the bookshelf sighing in relief
        darkness scratching at the door

it is the daydream
        the candle humming Nina Simone
        and tracing a gentle line around
        the room with a hot, sharp finger

it is the vagary
        the ideas stutter, embarrassed
        by the spotlight, and cover a cough
        loneliness strikes 4pm, carefully tearing the day
        in half

it is the nightmare
        the dregs and scalded genius stain
        the bottom of a chipped cup
        fool's gold

before the end

i am dancing slowly now
rolling out the curves and flowing now
i may pick up the pace before the end
but I have been frenetic eclectic magnetic
and while it pools around me like seafoam
it also makes me sweat
i like this measured swing this fling
it suits me now i wear it swell
and while i may pick up the pace
before the end,
my waltz knows things and knows them well
and now is my slow dance spell

SHORT STORIES

Whitney and the Joker
Amity Bradford

I loosened my tie and walked, head bowed, towards the training room. A rookie moved out of the way sheepishly and shot me a sympathetic glance. One chance left. I should have known this would happen. There isn't a lot of room for error here in the Academy. I slumped into my cubicle, laying my head heavy in my hands on my taupe laminate desk. I screw my eyes up tightly and exhale a long puff of air.

How was I supposed to know that Michaels was undercover?

I walked up to him in the stale cigarette, sweat infused club, clapping him on the back.
"HEY THERE, MICHAELS!" I boomed over the thump of the music.
His eyes widened slightly before closing slowly as if to transport himself somewhere else. I watched his fingers tighten, knuckles turning white around his sweating glass. His beer stuck haphazardly to the worn countertop, the suction resisting his grasp as he tried to lift it to his mouth. I've never seen any liquid fly like that before; right over Ricardo Delaware. The guy we've been trying to pin for ages on a cocktail of charges. I should have recognised him. I should have recognised Delaware. His hungry green eyes, cold and lifeless. His crimson scar, a deep divot in his left cheek, a bit like

The Joker, but only half committed to the look. Nothing about Delaware screamed 'ordinary civilian'. Even his beaten and fraying jacket was decorated with droplets of dried blood. How he has evaded arrest so far, I'm stumped.

Delaware leapt back, reflexively reaching into his left hip pocket. Rivulets of pale gold trailed down his face, pooling in the scarlet crevasse on his weathered face. His eyebrows hung low as he pivoted and ducked through the crowd towards the exit. He paused below the cold metal doorframe and scanned back to the swollen bar. His frosty eyes, piercing my own with an unmatched intensity. And just like that, Delaware had disappeared.

Grant Michaels leaned his large frame and his crossed arms on the ledge of my cubicle partitioning. He was the only constable that could make the partitions move with a single breath. The dude was a mountain.

"What were you thinking, man?" he said exasperated, with wild eyes.

I pulled my head from my hands and exhaled, turning my face up to his before I spoke.

"I fucked up. I'm sorry."

Michaels didn't disagree with me. Instead, he stared; his grey eyes boring into mine.

A ghost of a smile crept slowly onto his face, "You wanna make it up to me, rookie?".

I stammer out a fragmented 'yes'.

"Be at The Lincoln at 9. Just for some drinks", his voice light.

He turned and marched to his own cubicle, his

shoulders grazing both sides of the hallway. What the heck just happened? I sit at my desk, dumbfounded. I check my phone, 4:58pm. Looks like I'm going out tonight. I'm not about to let Michaels down for a second time if I want to keep my job. I'm just a rookie, goddammit.

I snatch my keys, wallet and phone. I check my holster and run my fingers over the hand engraved 'Whitney' on my trusty Glock 22 pistol. I pace towards the front exit. I need to get out of here. A single droplet of perspiration trails down my forehead. I swipe it away, annoyed.

"Hey, Dan! Before you go, I've got something for you!" Natalie cries out down the hall.

I stop in my tracks, grimacing, I turn back around and tread to her office next to reception.

Without waiting for me to enter her office, she begins talking, "… it's time for gun servicing, so you'll need to hand your pistol in, and I'll give you a replacement". She must have seen my face painted with shock and incredulity. "Relax, Dan, it's not like you're going to be unarmed. I am giving you a replacement," she said slowly as though she were talking to a spooked cat under a house. Seargent Peters walked by at that moment, glancing in, looking disappointed over his steel frame glasses. He must have heard about my little stunt. I pursed my lips and reached for Whitney and begrudgingly laid her gently on the table. I don't get attached to things. However, this gun is everything. It is the only thing I have left of my old man; a wedding present given to me when I married Whitney. He told me, Whitney might leave someday, but this gun never would.

Natalie clears her throat, the replacement black pistol outstretched to me; a questioning look on her face. In this moment my dad was wrong, they had both left. I hesitantly grab the new gun and toss it between my palms, feeling the unfamiliar weight of it for a moment before pocketing it in my holster. I give Natalie the nod of thanks and walk to the car park feeling like I've lost a limb. They've both left; my Whitneys. I shudder.

I arrive home and shower in my empty apartment. I wrap the towel tightly around my waist and stare into the smothered mirror. Aimlessly I wipe the condensation away and reveal an image of me. Bitter and stupid. Dumb. I ruined my career today. I run a calloused hand through my damp hair, letting the tangled strands flop down my forehead. I brace my hands on either side of the mirror and let my head hang, defeated. I should have recognised him. I should have recognised Delaware.

I plonk myself down on my single chair facing the television and turn on the news. Letting the usual talk of war, chemical warfare and Friday night footy games fill the solitary silence. I sit for what feels like hours, although it probably was only a few minutes. I check my phone, 8:51pm. Time to go. I tug on my scuffed boots and trudge down to The Lincoln, checking over my shoulder for something suspicious. Sometimes as a cop, you get the uneasy feeling that someone is watching you or paying extra attention to you. Call me paranoid, but it happens more than you'd think. I make my way past the graffitied crumbling brick wall and head towards the entrance. I forgot it was Halloween. After all, this is New York, you see people in questionable outfits all the time. Only this time, people have fewer clothes on although it is colder than a polar bears toenails out there. The line isn't long, and I nod at Gus. He waves me in without a second glance.

I take a deep breath and step over the threshold.

My eyes are assaulted with neon strobe lights and writhing bodies on the dance floor, almost possessed. I struggle to inhale the heady air, thick with sweat and carelessly spilt alcohol. I weave my way through the hordes of costume covered, or not covered patrons. Surely these people can afford real clothes. There isn't a barstool spare. Why did I venture out during Halloween? Oh, wait. Michaels.

I'm within arm's reach from the bar when Frankenstein's Bride taps me on the shoulder with a shiny, black taloned finger. I turn and face her, startled and creeped out by her stark, white eyes. The commitment to Halloween costumes is serious this year, no one is skimping on a costume; well, some are intentionally, but that's beside the point.

Frankenstein's Bride pokes lazily at my chest and slurs, "who are you suppo-ssed to be?".
She teeters to the right and sways to balance herself. She's almost fully gone. I've seen this exact thing before with Whitney. I shudder at the memory. I search her makeup caked face to gauge how she is going only to be met with white orbs and a collapsing monochrome hairdo as she crumples to the floor. Her

red death cocktail shatters onto the already sticky vinyl. She looks like she's been stabbed. By her cocktail, of course. Carmine splatters up the front of her torn wedding dress. I reach for her limp body and drag her off the floor. Zombies, vampires and nurses gape openly at the seemingly dead bride in my arms. I might be bitter and twisted, but I'm not that much of an arsehole that I'd leave a random chick to get trampled.

I find a quieter alcove with a spare seat where I dump her body, forcing the Hulk and a witch to untangle themselves and leave begrudgingly. She stirs, eyes fluttering still blank. Christ, I need a beer. I glance again at the limp bride propped against the grimy wall; milky eyes now frozen open. An inkling of familiarity surfaces, but I need a beer. Goodness knows I need it. She makes to move, and the claret stained white dress, tangles between her legs and she falls back dejected.

I finally weave through the throng of creatures to the bar. I order a much-needed beer and a red death cocktail to replace the one shattered on the vinyl. One good thing about this bar is that the drinks come quick. I glimpse towards the alcove and see Frankenstein's Bride staring at me intently with pale eyes. I raise my eyebrows with a nod to assure her I'm coming back with a drink for her. She grins, almost evil. Again, familiar, but I can't place it. I shake my head to remove the ghastly image of her devilish grin and translucent eyes and grab our drinks.

I manoeuvre into the seat opposite her, now vacant, trying not to slosh the vermilion concoction and my amber ale. I slide her drink across to her, and I make the mistake of making eye contact with her again. My entire body breaks out in a shiver. I get the feeling someone is watching me. I can't help it, alright.

My dad always said, 'It pays to be paranoid'. I look over my shoulder towards the bar and spot Superman and the Joker chatting happily by the classic bar. Halloween certainly brings everyone together; the good and the bad. The ghostly bride reaches for me across the table, knocking her drink. I'm not quick enough to catch it. The cardinal red quickly saturating my grey polo. Are you serious? This chick is smashed. I pull the wet fabric from my torso in disgust and stomp through the crowd to the bathroom.

The stain is a bitch to get out. But the time I get cleaned up Frankenstein's Bride is gone. I spot my beer right where I left it. Thank goodness for small miracles. I down it and wander to the bar for another. I can't see Michaels. It's nearly 10? He's obviously not coming. I might as well get hammered.

I don't get far, though. Frankenstein's Bride pushes me flat against a wall. Her face contorts angrily, and she drags my face down to hers, sharp talons gripping my collar. I freeze, my breathing suspended. I have been here before. I glance past her, silently pleading with a passing zombie for help. Instead, he smiles and gives me the universal 'lucky you' nod. I shift uncomfortably against the cold brick, avoiding her nails now encroaching on my jugular. My head spins. What? I've not even had like two beers tonight. I can't be sloshed already. My joints seize, and for a second, just a second, I am paralysed. I lengthen my neck as far as I can to give myself some room to breathe against the cage over my throat. I take a shaky breath and see Superman shake hands with The Joker and walk away. Michaels. Michaels is Superman.

I go to escape her grasp. I'm frozen. I try to move my fingers against my side. Paralysed. The Joker stalks towards us. I meet his gaze, hungry and piercing. I take a shaky breath as he reaches us, my eyes wide and terrified. The bloodstained bride kisses The Joker on the human side of his half-painted face. Everything clicks, including the gun, held against my torso. How could I not see this? It was blatantly obvious and staring me right in the face. I should have recognised him. I should have recognised Delaware. I should have recognised her.

Whitney.

Reflection

Caitlin Jankiewicz

She's messing with a spot on our forehead that only she and I can see. Every morning for the past two years it's been the same anxious routine. First, our forehead, which she pokes and prods then smears with greasy coverup. The end result looks worse, but she doesn't seem to realise that. Next, it's our eyes. This morning, I'm surprised when Grace pulls out her other makeup bag, the one she only uses on special occasions. I vaguely feel my stomach knotting, so I know hers must be doing the same. Our eyebrows knit as she layers gold eyeliner and eyeshadow across our eyelids, then carefully runs the mascara wand through our eyelashes. She has to start over twice because of the black smudges the unsteady wand leaves in the gold. The midwinter static leaves strands of her long blonde hair hanging in the air as she runs a brush through it and pulls it half up into a barrette. She grimaces at me when she's finally finished. From the other side of the glass I grimace back, wishing I could show her what she wants to see.

Grace doesn't remember the first time we saw each other, but I do. She was holding a spoon, partially covered with banana baby food. She laughed when she saw me, clownish in the distorted reflection. Another time, we saw each other in a puddle at the park. We smiled at our chubby cheeks and baby-blue eyes rimmed by a yellow raincoat hood. She tried to step on me, then accidentally sat down in the puddle. She cried the whole way home. We didn't see much of each other in those days, and she didn't think of me very often. We caught a glimpse of each other in a dusty compact mirror as she smeared pink lipstick across our face the day she found her mother's makeup bag, her guilty uncertainty filtering through the glass. Later, we shared a sheepish look in bathroom mirror as she sat on the sink, her mother scrubbing her face until it was almost the same shade as the lipstick. Another time she flashed me a smile when she noticed me in her father's glasses as he picked her up and tossed her in the air. When she was a bit older, we met each other in sparkly pink fairy costumes and gold crowns, twirling in her mother's wardrobe mirror. There was no fairy princess in the world more beautiful than us.

When Grace was 10, she went to school. Her mother had home schooled her until then, hoping to avoid the social culture of American schools, which took colourful, unique children, fed them through a complex machine of conformity and poppy trimming, and spat out perfectly square, uniform students. Grace arrived in 5th grade with the round tummy and messy hair of a child, and was greeted with a gaggle of miniature adults, girls who had been dieting for two years and had already started wearing makeup and having boyfriends. Grace quickly learned the social importance of a flat stomach and eye shadow. Slowly, we began to see more of each other. By the time 8th grade rolled around, she and I were checking in on each other between every class in the tiny magnetized mirror hanging in her locker. Although I tried my best, our shared smiles became rarer and rarer. Reflected behind her were the other girls in her class, adjusting their hair or touching up their lip gloss, each hoping to be the prettiest.

Today Grace is late to first period English, walking into class 40 seconds after the bell. I watch her from a glass bookcase in the front of the classroom as she hurries to her desk and settles her backpack at her feet. Around her, the only sound is that of pencils scratching on paper as the class scribbles furiously. The teacher hands her a test. I know she's ready for it. I've watched her study from her desk mirror for days, so I don't understand the butterflies careening in her stomach and the adrenaline running through her hands. She doesn't open the test, instead chewing on her pencil and casting sideways glances at someone the bookcase glass can't quite capture. Although she eventually starts writing, she checks her watch and glances to the side again every few minutes.

The bell rings, and the hallway fills as students burst from classrooms. The muddled fruity smell of perfume hangs on the air, lockers slam and shoes squeak on gritty linoleum floors. I watch Grace from glass trophy cases and classroom windows as she walks towards her locker, her head snapping around like a rabbit being hunted. A girl with long dark hair and olive skin at the locker next to Grace's swaps books from her locker before rooting around in her backpack for a hairbrush. A tall boy with dark hair walks by and winks at her. She looks up and smiles back. I feel Grace's stomach flip over as her heart skips a beat. She tucks her hair behind her ears and although I'm only faint in the glass, I can feel our cheeks flushing. The girl closes her locker and turns to Grace. I can't hear what the girls are saying, but the pasted smile on our face doesn't match the wistful longing in our eyes. The smile fades as the girl turns to leave.

I know Natalie well. I've seen her and her dark-haired reflection many times in the bathroom mirror, through the years that she and Grace have done their hair up, or played with multi-coloured thrift store eye shadow. Before that, I watched them dress up as pirates and gypsies, try on vintage screw-on earrings and 80's wigs, and line their eyes and lips with watercolour pencils. Grace and I were still smiling at each other back then, although there were also a lot of laughter at how ridiculous we looked.

Right before lunch, Grace and Natalie come into the girl's bathroom near the cafeteria.

"So…what did you want to tell me?" Grace's voice wobbles slightly.

Natalie's face is flushed as she answers, "Zack asked me out!"

I feel Grace freeze over inside as the breath is squeezed out of her lungs, "Oh…! What did you say?"

"I told him yes, obviously," Natalie squeaks in excitement, "I didn't even know he liked me!"

The muscles of my jaw clenches with Grace's. I realize that she's trying not to cry.

"That's awesome. I'm happy for you!" Grace's excited words are at war with the hollow cold inside her.

Natalie runs her fingers through her hair and grins, "Come on, let's go to lunch. He said he'd sit with us."

Natalie bounces through the door. Grace follows reluctantly, glancing back at me.

Is that anger in her eyes?

30 minutes later, Grace bursts through the

bathroom door and collapses on the floor. I can just barely see the top of her head in the mirror above the sink, unsteady as her body shudders with sobs. Silently, I beg her to come to me, to tell me what's wrong. Maybe, just maybe, she'll see me and smile, like she used to. After what seems like hours, she finally stands up and faces me in the mirror. Mascara is running down her cheeks in dirty rivulets. She scrubs at it with a piece of paper towel, smudging it across her flushed face.

"I hate you," she whispers to me.
She splashes cold water on her face, washing away the streaks of black, then looks back at me. I can't tell if the tears in my eyes are hers or my own.

I don't see Grace for the rest of the day. In the darkness, the space between reflections, the words ricochet like bullets. She hates me. How can she hate me? I've known her for her entire life. There hasn't been a day the she's lived that I haven't been there with her.

I am her.

I step out of the shower and wrap myself with a towel. In the fogged-up mirror, my reflection stares back at me. My wet hair is slicked back away from my face, which is red and patchy from the hot water, and smudged mascara lingers around my eyes. I'm graduating high school today. I think back to that day in the bathroom, two years ago, when Natalie and Zack first started dating. Now, with my raccoon eyes and red face, I don't look all that different. I hurriedly wash the mascara off in the sink. I'd known Zack liked Natalie for months, but that didn't stop me hoping that he might still notice me. I'd hated myself back then. I'd wanted Zack to choose me, to prove that I was worth a guy's notice, that I was pretty enough for him. The steam on the mirror has cleared up slightly. I fluff up my hair so it covers my ears and look at my face in the mirror. The person I see has worked hard, and is graduating at the top of her class. She's made friendships that will last a lifetime, and has big plans for the future. I meet the eyes of my reflection. They're my father's eyes. My hair is my mother's. My nose and face shape are my aunt's. My grandpa gave me my lips and chin. All the people who love me stare back at me from the mirror. I know how proud of me they all are. I may not love myself yet, but they do. Maybe, for now, that's enough. I smile slightly.

My reflection smiles back.

The Breeze

Lachlan Bilson

The breeze is rising again. As always it starts with a moan. Before the faintest breath of air brushes our cheeks I can hear it way off, whining itself through the catacombs. Soon it will reach us, breaching the cavern through tunnelled constrictions to dance and shriek amongst the stalactite above the spring lake's shore, before descending with death's stench and a chill like sharpened stone. It is always the same when the breeze rises, we the dwellers fervently flee from it as it assaults our senses and reason. We know it is inevitable; it will eventually consume us.

I try not to focus on the sound. The moan of the breeze is growing to a shriek, but it is still distant, she still has time. I focus on Athena, my hand pressed to her back as she sleeps next to me, coiled on the stone, assured of my protection. I draw warmth through her calloused skin and bone, count her breaths through the contour of her shoulders, and feel her blood dragging itself through her veins.

I wish I were less selfish. Athena would want to be awake before the breeze came. The silence is already gone and will not be returning in time. She would still want to breathe cleanly before the stench's descent and feel air on her skin before it is sharpened by the chill, but I cannot bear to watch what would happen next, to see her deteriorate. Even asleep, the sound of the breeze's distant moan is pooling salt on her skin.

I am imagining waking her; the hand place on her back would clench to dig nails so slightly onto her skin. She would sigh herself into consciousness, uncoiling with a shudder as she became aware of the sound heralding the approach of the unknowing, unyielding assailant. Her shoulders would contort more rapidly, her breaths rasp more fiercely as she'd reach out for me, finding and clasping the bone beneath my arm to ask, "How long?"

"Not long."

The sound is getting closer now, it seems as though its advancement is too gradual to wake her, or perhaps she does not really want to be awake, does not want to see what happens next. I can hear the frenzy of the other Dwellers as they scramble along the water's shale edge caring not to fall in, reaching for one another and huddling for heat and for safety. I would wake Athena to join them now, but after what I've done, they will never accept our warmth.

If I had woken her, she would be able to hear the eruption now, the screech of the breeze bursting into the cavern from the tunnels and cavities around. Her breaths would still be rapid, but now they would also be deep as she desperately pursued each clean wisp before it was stolen from her by the smell of decay. She would want to be awake for this, she would not want to miss it. She would breath deeper and deeper until the moment before the last, when I would yell, "Hold," and we would seal our lungs shut, refusing to relinquish the last taste until it went stale in our mouths.

The scuffling of the dwellers around me has stopped, they hold their breaths as we would have done. I have learnt to not fight submission, I let the scent fill me, corrupt me, corrode me from the inside. Beside me, still asleep, Athena gags. Moments pass before the dwellers around us collectively take their first breath of dead air, then cry out wordlessly as one cacophonous choir, their chorus near rising above the screech in the air. I take the time to do what needs to be done.

If I had woken Athena, we would have joined in the cries, but hers would have lasted longer than any other. Each time the breeze rises it leaves less of her behind, and now there was little left. Her sigh would have become an erratic sob until she could not make a sound through the shivering as the chill finally descending upon us.

The other dwellers were quiet now, grouped for warmth, but they will not let me in and they would not have let her in. If I had woken her, she would be near convulsions now as the warmth was stripped from her body. I do not know how she would have tried to escape; I am imagining that she would have pulled herself between stone crevasses, sheltering from the breeze and exposing herself to the sharp shale that cuts even deeper. If I had woken her, I wouldn't have been able to listen to her suffer, her skin grate along the rock. I would have done anything to stop it. I would have led her to the lake.

The lake is the centre of the cavern, its warmth being drawn from beneath the stone, and though the air is cold, its warmth makes this place more liveable than anywhere in the world above. If I had woken her, I would have led her into the lake and together we would have waded out until we could barely reach the stone below. We would have still smelled the stench, the decay, we wouldn't have been able to avoid it, but we would be warm. We would slow our breathing as warm vapour filled our lungs, and she would stretch on her back submerging her ears beneath all sound. There we would stay for some time, ignoring the understanding that we had sealed our fates.

Warm water is an addiction from which you cannot escape and if I had woken her, I would watch it consume her as it consumed me. Time would draw itself thin as we hid underneath soft ripples, but eventually we would have to rise, and the breeze's dancing cry would torture us so much more now that we had experienced release from it. Motivated by starvation or exhaustion we would pull ourselves onto the stone shore, but before we dried, the warm water on us would turn to ice in the breeze. I imagine Athena shuddering, trying again and again to pull herself onshore before being driven back in by the sting. To choose between dying and being unable to live. Even if eventually she did find the strength to pull herself to shore, and to stay, she would have been too weak, too late to save herself.

The breeze stopped much faster than I expected it too, fading quickly, and the chill had barely reached us. She would have wanted to be awake, she would have wanted me to wake her. The only sound is a dripping from the stone in my hand. I couldn't listen to her suffer, I couldn't let it happen. Athena's blood wasn't dragging itself through her veins anymore, her shoulders had gone still as the Dwellers cried after the last clean breath, and I carried her to the mouth of the catacomb tunnels from which the breeze came.

Excerpt from Suburbia

Sally-Mae Herford

The time on Paul's dark grey Ford Ranger dashboard clock read ten-to-seven as he reversed out of his single space driveway in the heart of Sydney's Tamarama. It was Mother's Day Sunday, and he hoped to beat the early morning traffic which would inevitably be plaguing the roads in the next hour. Paul tightened his grip on the steering wheel with his left hand while rubbing the sleeplessness out of his eyes with the other. Glancing in the rear-vision mirror, he examined the short blond hair he had meticulously styled in the ten minutes before leaving his house. Enthusiastic joggers scattered the footpaths, attempting to catch the morning rays that streamed between the apartment buildings. Paul's muscles ached in jealousy. If it weren't for this disruption in his ritualistic exercise schedule, Paul would be reaching his 20th km in his daily 25km run. Paul tried not to think about the lost progress as he slowed to a stop at a red traffic light.

A young girl in a white Suzuki Swift pulled up beside him. Profanity-filled music blared through the thick car doors of the hatchback. Paul smirked in her direction as the girl played with the mousey hair that fell from a messy bun atop her dainty head. Her tight McDonalds uniform looked well-used, most likely from a long night shift. Paul attempted to guess her age. Her ambiguous figure suggested that it could have ranged from seventeen to twenty-five. It was impossible to tell these days. Paul had been caught out countless times with girls like this. They coated their faces with cheap makeup and paired it with tight clothing that caused their prepubescent bodies to bludge out, making it impossible to deduce whether they'd even graduated high school. In reality, they were still getting their mums to top up their Opal cards for weekends. Paul would have to back off when their tradie boyfriends would come charging in like angry sheepdogs, hollering about their age, as if it ever stopped them. The light turned green, and Paul left the girl in a cloud of tailgate fumes.

Mentally calculating his time, Paul deduced that he could pick up everything he needed from Bunnings in about forty-five minutes, make it home, start on the project and have the whole thing done by the time Ten News came on at five. Perhaps the completion of this project would finally show Grace that he wasn't so useless around the house after all. Paul felt the hunger-pains that had gone ignored for the last twenty-four hours return in his lower abdomen, this time with an increasing vengeance. He wished Grace would make something worth consuming. The countless meals he had gracefully suffered through to spare an argument reminded him of how much he could withstand. Recently, Paul felt as though she had been trying to poison him. After he finished this job, she'd think twice about putting the cheap full-cream milk in his coffee instead of his Nutty Bruce Organic Activated Almond Milk.

The ocean-like Bunnings car park had fewer cars than he had expected and he pulled into the disabled spot closest to the entrance. Paul, once again, checked his hair in the rear-vision mirror, unbuckled his seat belt and swung open his driver's door hopping down onto the, slowly warming, concrete. An unmemorable over-weight female sales assistant gave him a suspiciously excited smile as he walked through the automated entrance doors. That smile, he had seen countless times before.

Grace always wore it each time Paul returned home, hours past knock-off time. That disingenuous smile always put him on edge, as though she was trying to hide something, she didn't want him to discover. And her efforts to accommodate his attempts for a greeting kiss made it seem like he made it a chore for her. Her face clearly wincing at the aroma of his breath.

He didn't return the favour to the sales assistant; his mind was already scoping out the exact aisles he would need to visit to get everything he needed for the day's work. He claimed a shopping cart pushed to the side of the aisle, abandoned by its previous owner, too lazy to return it to its home. Paul stood in the middle of the main aisle, scanning the aisle numbers and their contents as people walked around him. Towards the end of the warehouse, he spotted it "Garden Care" and hastily pointed his empty trolley in that direction. Paul passed a variety of aisles with a multitude of home and hardware contents; his eyes fell on a half-priced sales shelf that read "Stanley fibreglass claw hammers". The exact hammer he'd bought five years previously when they'd just moved to Tamarama.

Grace had said they were going to need one if they were going to assemble any furniture. He knew she had meant children's furniture. At first, the comments made by Grace's colleagues at her school about 'settling down' were mixed in with their usual humorous dinner table banter. Those, once so innocent comments had begun to seep further into the cracks of her mind and became fuel for weekly arguments that conveniently fell on every Friday night after work, allowing their grievances to fester and stir all weekend. Both individuals would then return to work on Monday morning tense and emotionally sore from their weekend ritual.

Paul reached his desired destination, pushed his trolley into aisle four and began to scour the shelves. With his stomach now settled, Paul remembered the throbbing in his hands. He paused, attempting to rub the stiffness out of them and pulled his long sleeve shirt down to conserve warmth as he gripped the trolley handle. Amongst the general noises of a busy warehouse Paul could faintly hear the store speakers overhead playing Coldplay's famous 2000 hit "Yellow".

Paul remembered those romantic lyrics playing softly through Grace's car speakers the night they had both attempted a spontaneous date after a long period of minimal physical contact. The weekly scheduled arguments between the two had now festered into complete and utter radio silence for over half a year. The couple had put on happy faces for the relatives during the seasonal holiday get-togethers, however, once all the turkey and wine had been consumed and the family members returned home, the familiar silence would make itself at home again. Paul remembered how beautiful Grace had looked that night, in her deep maroon wrap dress. It had been so long since he had seen her in anything other than work clothes or track pants. He remembered how the deep red had complimented her smooth porcelain skin, a colour she had come to wear a lot more in the recent days.

Paul eyes finally rested on the items he had so meticulously researched online before leaving the house that morning. As he began ensuring the quality of his item, he saw out of the corner of his eye, a Bunning's sales assistant walking down the aisle towards him. Paul hadn't come here with the intension of talking to anyone; his thorough research ensured him that he knew exactly what he needed. In one swift movement, Paul positioned his back on the boy and tried to look busily at the items on the shelf. Discombobulated, the boy stood in silence for a few seconds before turning his attention towards an elderly woman further down the aisle that seemed to be struggling with her trolley. Paul turned his attention back to his job, effortlessly pulled two 25kg bags from the shelves, one in each arm and dumped them in his trolley. Paul pushed his trolley out of aisle four and started towards aisle eight in hopes of finding the last item on his list. A feeling of exhilaration came over him. The assistants look of shock and confusion was the same expression he had seen on Grace so recently.

Paul had suspected for three months that Grace was being unfaithful. He couldn't be entirely sure, but Grace had begun a habit of return home well past her usual time. Paired with the arrival of a new ex-NRL PE teacher who sported neck muscles the width to his head, this lateness made Paul quite sure that he had been replaced by a younger, dumber, and more muscular version. At first, he pushed the suspicions to the furthest corners of his mind, reminding himself that Grace would never be able to hide a secret like that; but the more he ignored them, the more undeniable they felt. The evidence had burrowed into his mind without permission, laying eggs of suspicion about everything Grace said or did. One particular Thursday night after Paul had found companionship at the bottom of eight premium Canadian Clubs, Grace returned home from supposed 'drinks with friends' with the remains of the red lipstick she'd left the house wearing smeared across her cheek, Paul finally found what came after the end of his patience. It was as if she had snuffed out the remaining ambers of their once burning relationship. He now saw Grace for who she really was and what she was capable of and in return, what he was truly capable of. And that look, that look of shock and disbelief on her face when she realised made him laugh, even now.

Paul reached aisle eight now and was sorting through the various options available for his final purchase. Picking up the one he had seen advertised for half price on the website, Paul made sure the in-store price was the same before laying it in his trolley and making his way to the checkout. Paul lined up behind a young mother with a toddler attached to her hip and a shopping cart full of half-priced potted flowers. Paul noticed the remnants of breakfast stuck to the toddler's rosy cheeks; its tiny fingers wrapped around a filthy, stuffed creature. Its limbs were flailing around as its mother attempted to prop it higher on her hip. Distracted by Pauls presence, the child lost grip of the stuffed creature, and it fell to the concrete floor. The toddler let out a piercing cry as the mother quickly tried to hush it, not noticing the dropped toy. Paul stared straight ahead, pretending not to know the solution to the mother's embarrassment. The woman continued, in vain, to quieten the child as more people began to look in her direction. She hastily paid for her items and pushed her trolley out of the store, now sporting the same red-cheeked appearance as the hysterical toddler. Paul, next-in-line to pay, placed his items on the bench as the young female sales assistant began scanning their barcodes.

"So just the two bags of lime and shovel today, sir?"

Paul nodded as he reached into his back pocket for his wallet and pulled out his credit card.

"Your total comes to $67.80; how would you like to pay for that?"

Paul held up his credit card; the girl pressed a few

buttons on her checkout screen.

"Just tap or insert when you're ready." She said, motioning towards the eftpos machine between them. Paul quickly tapped his card on the eftpos machine.

"Get into a big one last night ay?" the girl asked nodding her head in the direction of Pauls knuckles, all blistered and swollen.

Paul quickly pulled the long sleeve shirt down past them before answering, "You could say that."

Till Death do us Part

Kathryn Staples

He never thought the chills would shake his body like a high magnitude earthquake. His teeth were hitting each other over and over, making the annoying chattering sound so often heard in cartoons. Even the heat from two singlets, a long sleeve t-shirt, a woollen jumper and a trench coat could not stop the tremors. John tried to capture as much warmth as he could manage, sinking back into the weathered, washed-out blue leather chair. His prison for the next two hours. Closing his eyes, he wrapped his arms around his torso, being careful to make sure not to pull out the IV slowly releasing poison into his bloodstream. He took in a deep breath and clean, sanitised air filled his lungs. He hated the smell of disinfectant; the fumes burned his nose with every intake.

"I got you another blanket babe." John was met with the deep, warm brown, smiling eyes of his husband Michael as a thin hospital blanket settled peacefully over his lap. It did little to hold the tremors at bay, but he couldn't tell his husband that.

"Thank you, my love," he whispered. John gave his husband a weak smile, all that he could manage while trying to hide the teeth chattering. Sitting there in the uncomfortable armchair, he wondered how his husband could still be so happy in this situation.

"Well, would you look at that! Seems I went

through all the trouble of bringing you a blanket for nothing!" The small nurse chuckled, tucking the unneeded blanket under her arm. She was a short woman in her late fifties to early sixties, her dyed orange hair glowing under the harsh fluorescent lights.

"Sorry, Jenifer seems my husband has overstepped again." He gave a cheeky glare to his husband. Reaching out and grabbing his husband's hand, John let out a small chuckle and leaned his head onto his shoulder. Michael's thumb made small gentle half-moon circles on the back of John's hand, a motion that always comforted him no matter the situation.

"It's so nice to see such a beautiful couple," Jenifer chuckled. She checked the IV line to make sure everything was transferred before she disconnected and pulled it out, a sting shooting up his arm as she did so.

"I know I'm beautiful, but Michael's looking a little haggard these days." Laughing, John rubbed his hand where the needle had left just a moment ago, now tender and pulsing, before he folded up the blanket. He planted a kiss on his husband's cheek, and Michael responded by sliding his arms around his shoulders. The pressure was light; the action careful as if handling a small animal. He knew his husband was just trying to be considerate; he knew he was much weaker than before. He was well aware of his collarbone hollow growing more profound by the day. He knew his cheekbones were more prominent, and he looked like he had not slept in over a week. John knew all of this, but it still hurt; all he wanted was to be treated the same. He was not so fragile that he would break just from his husband's touch.

"Thank you again, Jenifer. These hospital trips are always easier when you are on." John handed the folded blanket over, Jenifer gliding soundlessly past the sleeping patients to put both blankets back in the cupboard.

"You boys take care now and don't get up to too much mischief," her lips curled up sweetly, lipstick bleeding out past her lip line as she did so.

"I'll make sure to keep him out of trouble." His husband gave him a cheeky wink as he tugged softly on his arm, leading him through the large double doors into the waiting room. Giving a small wave goodbye to the receptionist as they walked by her desk, the warm sunlight washed over them as the automatic door opened to the outside. Climbing into the back of the medium white sedan, Michael pushed the start button on the control panel pressed into the back of the centre console. They were greeted with a smooth female voice welcoming them, asking where they would like to go.

"Take us home," Michael commanded the car.

It slowly backed out of the spot before blending seamlessly into the flow of traffic on the main road. After every session of chemo, John felt weak and tired; he could feel the poison attacking and destroying the cells in his body.

"Did you want anything on our way home?"

Michael was always so caring, asking the same question week after week as if he was going to give a different answer.

"Nuh, I just want to go..."

He could not finish his sentence, a cough racking through his body. His throat burned, his chest tight and tears filled his eyes. The struggles to get air into his lungs left him more breathless, panic setting in. He put his head between his knees, trying to focus his mind on breathing in and out. He felt circles being rubbed into his back, and he was handed a brown paper bag. Taking deep breaths, he began to calm down slowly, his burning lungs cooling down as the pressure melting away.

"It's getting worse I think…" Concern was written all over Michael's face.

"No… we are not talking… about this again," he cut his husband off sternly, taking a deep breath in-between each set of words.

He turned his head away, watching the cars speeding past the window. He didn't want to have this argument again. He had to put on a brave face and act as if everything about the situation didn't bother him. He hated the 'look' that people gave when they saw a sick person; he hated the way his husband looked at him. The only thing he seemed to see was a sick man.

An advertisement rolled across a passing white van interrupting his train of thought—the bright pulsing colours grabbing his undivided attention.

"Gods Breath, Have A New Lease On Life," He muttered angrily.

The cure to cancer only available to the filthy rich Clenching his fist until his knuckles turned white John tore his gaze away from the taunting words. He would never be able to afford the miracle; his husband had already looked into every way possible to obtain it. The van pulled away replaced by a B-double truck advertising plastic surgery, the pulsing neon image of an old lady transforming into a young and beautiful woman.

"What's going through your mind, honey?" Michael spoke softly, breaking him out of his trance.

"Do you think they are happier after they get plastic surgery?" He pointed out the window.

"I think they will be for a while, but it doesn't take the years away. They will still eventually die."
His voice dropped almost to a whisper at the end. Johns insides squeezed, his mouth tasted of copper, and his body broke out into goosebumps every time death was mentioned. He couldn't accept his fate. Not when there was a cure just out of his reach. John looked back out the window, Michael sheepishly turned away. He knew that he was causing his husband to worry, but the topic of death was off-limits.

There was a soft blue glow being emitted from under the letterbox as the car pulled into the driveway.

"I'll get the mail" he muttered sliding out of the seat. Michael gave a small 'okay' as acknowledgement. He knew he was being immature over such a little thing. He crudely tore open the envelope addressed to him; noting the doctor's name that ran across the paper.

Dear John Stone,

There have been some developments made in your treatment. Please call Dr Redtree at your earliest convenience.

Kind Regards,
Eden Medical Centre

His palms began to sweat and his hands shook, making it almost impossible to fold the letter back up. A shiver slivered its way down his spine and to the furthest tips of his body leaving behind tiny bumps in its wake. He managed to hide the letter in the inside pocket of his trench coat. He didn't want his husband to see it; it could only mean trouble. A million thoughts fought to become the centre of his attention, none of them good.

"What's wrong, honey?" Michael looked up from his tablet concerned, the tea he had just been stirring, swirled clockwise in the mug. The tea bag stained the water a deep brown.

"The rates and car insurance have come in," This small lie wouldn't hurt him. He dropped the bills on the kitchen counter before picking up his hot mug of fresh tea. Michael scoffed and muttered inaudibly as he settled into his black leather armchair.

"Sam and George left a message to make sure that we can still make it to dinner with them tonight, " Michael looked over his mug with a questioning expression.

"We have been putting dinner off for too long. Let's go." He smiled partly from the joy of the warm mug heating his frozen fingers, and partly a lie to hide his unwillingness to go out.

"Shall I run a bath for us to relax a bit before we go?" Michaels smile was infectious. He looked like a teenager eager for some alone time. The joy in his voice made John feel worse; all he wanted to do was find out what the doctor had to say about his treatment.

"No, it's okay, you have a shower first, I've done nothing but sit around. You're the one that has been running around after me all day." He leaned over and gave his husband a small kiss on the cheek. Michael chuckled, shaking his head in agreement.

He swirled the tea around in the mug. He had no appetite for drinking. Michael kissed his forehead and took the cup from him, placing it in the sink on his way to the bathroom. John waited until he could hear the water running before he ran to the study. Dialling the number into the control panel on the wall he heard it ring once, twice, five times. His nerves sent the butterflies in his stomach into a frenzy.

"Hello, Mr Stone. Thank you for contacting me so quickly." The doctor's voice was smooth and calm."Your application for the cure has been carefully evaluated." The doctor took a deep breath centering himself. There was no expression in his voice.

"Unfortunately, your application has been denied due to insufficient funds and lack of assets to put up as insurance," the doctor paused only for a second.

"Your chemo treatment will continue as normal. However, the addition of radiotherapy will be added to the off weeks of your chemo." John didn't have time to reply; the doctor ended the call after a quick, 'Goodbye'.

John's legs lost tension, collapsing under him and causing him to fall into the large padded office chair. His breathing was quick and shallow, his chest constricting with every intake. He tasted salt on his lips, warm liquid flowing down his cheeks without permission, creating dark wet dots over his blue jeans. He couldn't feel his body; there was no weight, all his limbs were numb with the realisation of impending death. He needed to wash his face, calm the redness in his eyes before his husband noticed.

Looking in the mirror, an unrecognisable face stared back at him: chapped pale lips, sunken cheeks and a receding hairline. He was just thankful that he hadn't lost all of his hair. Turning away with a sigh, he pulled on a new pair of jeans, now loose around the waist and buckled up his belt. He sat on the edge of the bed, and he looked down at his empty shoes waiting to be filled. As he reached down his mouth began to salivate, his stomach filling with butterflies. He quickly covered his mouth and shot up; however, his vision blurred, his head spun, and he fell back onto the bed. He looked everywhere to find something, anything before it was too late. It was already building up; he could taste the foulness on his tongue. Tears began to roll down his cheeks; he couldn't hold it anymore.

"It's okay I have the bucket!" Michael screamed. His vision filled with the blue container just as the contents of his empty stomach dribbled down the sides. The convulsions kept pushing his stomach until nothing more came out and the bile burned his throat.

"Thank... Thank you, my love," He panted. He collapsed forward nearly landing into the bucket, but his husband's strong arms caught him and supported his weight instead.

"I don't think we should be going out tonight..." Michael wiped the corner of John's lips with his towel, concern laced in his voice.

"No, I will be fine," he smiled reassuringly as he gave his husbands arm a weak squeeze. "Let's go. I'm looking forward to going out tonight. Can you help me put my shirt on, though?" His husband laughed, agreeing while he took the bucket out of the room. John smiled to himself; he would keep this a secret.

The Glasshouse

Calum Entermann

Thick columns of dark emerald towered above Dylan as he walked the length of the warehouse. He eyed them with awe and ran his fingertips along one of the vertical stacks - a habit he'd indulge when other tradesman weren't around. He mused on the city buildings and sky-scrapers these enormous panes would one day clad. Like tall sentinels in clear chainmail. The glass felt cold and smooth to touch. Each stack was like a giant block of translucent marble. Each in need of a Michelangelo to form them into something grand like the London Shard, or a Louvre pyramid. Dylan imagined the names shining on the recognition plaque of each edifice and replaced them with his own.

The squeal of the glass furnace pulled him out of his daydream and rang out along the breezeway. The factory was a shed the size of a football field with openings each end large enough for two semi-trailers to drive right through the middle. He felt a gust of wind from the west entrance nip at his bare legs as he walked back to the loading bay. The low sun pried through the entryway and he could feel the winter solstice approaching as his teeth chattered with cold.

The noise boomed again from the southern wing of the building. The loading bay occupied the northern wing where he worked. Here, the glass stood in heavy rows until trucks came to receive the fragile pallets and haul them across the land to job sites.

As he approached his work station, he could see Steve, his tall, buzz cut supervisor in the middle of an animated exchange with a delivery driver.

"Can't you just cut 'em down to size?"
"It's toughened glass – that's what you ordered, isn't it?"
"Yeah"
"Well you can't cut toughened glass,"
"Why not?"
"It's been tempered. It'll shatter"
"You said it was the strongest glass on the market."
"It is - You could whack it with a hammer all day– it won't break. But try cut it down, or ding one of the corners and she busts. That's her kryptonite."
"That's ridiculous"
"It's just science, mate."
"Three milimeters too big?!"
"Come back tomorrow morning, we'll have 'em all redone."
"I drove an hour and a half to get here."
"Sorry mate"
"Bloody hell"
The driver muttered and turned away.
Dylan made eye contact with Steve. They watched the man huff over to his parked truck.

Steve shrugged to Dylan, "Some muppet cut his order of thirty panels three millimeters' oversize. Now that's what not to do, alright greeny?"

"Measure twice, cut once"

"Never forget it."

"I won't"

"Good man." He planted a pair of yellow rubber gloves against Dylan's chest, "Take those oversize panels all to the skip bin outside. Don't make a mess."

"Righto Steve-o," Dylan chimed as he turned.

He looked down at his hi-vis vest and smiled to himself. Out of all the glass types, toughened was his favorite to work with. If his training was any indication, he'd become an expert in breaking glass long before doing anything productive with it. He was still amazed at the sheer amount of stock that was thrown to the tip, all because of little mistakes like these.

Dylan walked over to the stack of toughened glass by the loading bay, dug his fingernails between the first sheet to break the suction between the panels. Then with two hands on each side, he bent his knees and lifted the panel. It had been five months since he had started his apprenticeship, his first job. Carrying these panels used to feel like hell but today he could feel his shoulder-muscles building, his arms no longer felt like they were going to be ripped out of their sockets and he could finish the whole stack without needing a break. He felt proud of his progress.

He continued ferrying the glass back and forth from the loading bay to the skip bin outside. One pane at a time. He didn't mind this type of work, repetitive and physical. He lost himself in the rhythm.

Soon he was breathing heavily and the right side of his face slid against the glass with sweat. As he rounded the east entryway towards the skip bin, a cool nor-easterly picked up. The wind pooled against the glass and he found himself struggling to walk straight. The wind started rotating him on the spot against his will and he felt like one of those windsocks at the airports. He remembered the clear words of his TAFE instructor, "there are two types of weather to watch for in the glass business. Hail and wind. Hail is your friend and will turn your business into an overnight success. But wind is your enemy. Without warning it will turn your windowpanes into kites."

He stood on the spot with his legs wide apart, his grip slipping on the glass. Once the wind subsided, he rushed the pane the last meters to the skip. He'd learnt to handle the glass with utmost care as he carried each piece to the bin, lifted it overhead head and placed it horizontally on the rim. He'd also learnt to throw the pane lengthways to the back-left corner of the skip, halfway down to avoid a shower of glass fragments rebounding back out. He grabbed the sheet with two hands, aimed and heaved the glass away. Despite a firm shove, the pane didn't break on impact, which happened more often than he thought possible. The first time it happened, he ignored it and continued to throw more glass in on top. That week the garbage truck had to be called in early to empty the bin and the glass wedged in place proved difficult to break. The boss was livid. Since then, Dylan quickly learned to keep his hammer on a tool belt around his waist.

Now taking the hammer in his right hand, Dylan placed his left hand on the metal rim. In one deft motion, he threw his legs up, grabbed hold of the upright bin lid and then crouching down on the edge, he peered in. With his other hand on the adjacent edge, he lowered himself inside, landing beside the unbroken panel and on old iced-coffee cartons. He could smell the curdled milk and before he had the mind to move his feet, he felt something cold leak through the hole of his left boot. He winced and shuffled back until his spine pressed against the bin wall. With the panel at knee height, he took the hammer and lined it up with the nearest corner of the unbroken pane. No matter how many times he did this he felt an odd feeling in his stomach, like he was about to pop a balloon inside a cathedral at Mass. Steeling himself, he drew the hammer back two inches and gently tapped the corner. The glass turned to a thousand pebbles and fell down the gaps and holes between the junk. He felt some land down his boots. The glass made soft clicking sounds as fragments continued to split and release tension. Like a sigh. As if every pane of glass waits for the day it's broken.

He was tempted to stay in there listening to the particles like smashed ice trickling down blades of grass in a park. The sound of an end to something.. The sweet smell of rotten milk and the sound of an approaching vehicle quelled the thought and he began hauling himself up to the rim.

Swinging his legs over and sitting on the edge, he saw one of the old tradesmen coming past on the forklift with a pallet of thick glass sheets standing upright and on a slight lean back over the cab. Steve walked alongside to be his eyes. Dylan nodded to Steve who was too engrossed to notice. Dylan wished he could drive the forklift and use the glass on it to make something impressive. There must have been at least forty sheets of it in the slab. He imagined breaking it down, heating it in a fiery blaze, watching the orange-white glow of it as it morphed into something new. Still in his thoughts, he got up and began to tightrope along the mouth of the bin. Another gust of wind pushed at his side and he launched his body off to avoid falling back inside. He landed hard in a low crouch and a piece of glass bit deep into his left heel.

He swore loudly as he rolled backwards clutching his foot. The forklift lurched to a halt and both men looked over their shoulders toward the sound.

The wind caught the glass on the forklift in its airy hands and pushed it past its vertical lean. It tottered forward and over the point of balance. The slab bore down over Steve and swallowed him in one smooth motion. A dull popping sound came from underneath as the glass landed horizontal without a bounce. Not a single pane broke in the fall and now there was a two-inch gap between the lowest sheet and the concrete. Space enough for a man, or the tunneling wind.

No shatter of broken glass. Just the whirr of the furnace and the cooling turbines from inside the factory.

The old man streamed profanities as he wrestled his seat belt.

Dylan looked up from his foot and saw the fallen pallet.

Forgetting his cut, he got up and started running to the men, fumbling for the hammer on his belt as he went. His legs began to buckle as he approached the green slab. He dropped to his knees and started pushing at the first sheet of glass. He pushed hard and the glass edge dug into the skin of his palms. He could see Steve under it all, magnified through the green film, face down. Dark oil-like liquid leaking from his body. A life-sized microscope slide like laminated leaf sample from biology class.

"Shit! Push it off the poor bugger! Push!" the old man wheezed.

The sheets were vacuumed tight together and would not budge. Dylan wrestled the hammer from his tool belt and swung the head sideways into the closest corner of glass. His view of Steve vanished as the sheet fractured white. Dylan kept swinging, each one aimed to connect with the exposed corners of the next pane down. "Come on!" he yelled at the glass.

He continued in a frenzy until the panels disappeared under the mound of shattered pieces. Then he scooped large handfuls of the graveled glass to the side until the corner resurfaced. He bled and bashed at the glass again and again. Eventually, he reached the final sheet. As the hammer made contact, the whole mound dropped the remaining two inches to the ground. Glass pieces flew up in his face as air pockets escaped from underneath.

The sun was setting. An upright stack of glass in the west entryway grabbed the sunlight by the throat and threw it across the warehouse. The reflection lay strewn up the high wall on the east side. Shouts increased as more tradesmen ran to the scene. Soon he'd hear the sirens coming in the distance. The flashing lights and uniforms would make it official. He looked down. Under a mountain of crystals, each a perfectly formed miniature of itself, the broken shards of a man lay in a crumbled heap, glass-grains sticking to him like sand. Blood diamonds glistening in the evening sun.

What Next

Ashley Cotter

Nothing about her really stood out - in fact, I wouldn't have even noticed her if she hadn't shouted "Hi!" directly at my face in the crowded bar. I glanced to my right and around before she said it again.

"Hi! What whiskey are you drinking? That's what I've got too."

She tipped her glass toward mine, and I gave her drink a hesitant clink with my own. I wasn't annoyed… more intrigued, actually. This girl might not have stood out in a crowd, but her smile, when it was pointed at you, made you lose track of time, like anything was possible.

She shouted something else, but her voice got carried away by the movement of people. The bar was packed for a late Thursday afternoon, filled with black denim and groomed beards and well-placed piercings, each person trying to stand out the same way as everyone else. I myself was dressed in all black, yesterday's stubble on my face and a worn Levi's jacket thrown over my shoulder in the heat of people. I think the only thing that made me different from the black-cladded mob in this place was the fact I was holding a whiskey and not whatever hoppy IPA sloshed in the pint glasses in everyone's hands.

The girl gave me another smile and gestured toward the patio on the roof. I stepped out to follow her, feeling relief at the hit of fresh air.

"I'm Ally," the girl grinned in the outside quiet, taking a sip of her whiskey. "What's your name?"

"Sam," I answered, noticing for the first time she was dressed like she wasn't from here. Her jeans hugged her legs and were well-worn, but like they were her favourite pair, not freshly thrifted from one of the dozens of over-priced vintage shops in the area. Her boots looked like they'd been places; her white tee cropped, showing the faintest hit of skin above the waistline of her pants. She kept tucking her unruly brown hair behind her ears, an attempt to tame the wildness that I would later come to associate with her.

We watched pink streak the sky behind the cityscape views on the bar's rooftop. I was sceptical about this girl that popped out of nowhere, but was hooked on her energy.

"This kind of light makes me feel alive." Ally leaned back and shut her eyes, golden rays hitting her face. "You know?"

"I think so." And I think I did, just from looking at her.

"How did you end up in this city?" She genuinely wanted to know.

I paused, considering the nature, the culture, the job opportunities.

"You know, one day, I passed through on my way to visit some buddies down south, and something about the place just drew me in. I just knew this is where I needed to be."

She looked directly at me as I said this, and I knew she got it in a way my friends didn't. They had all been born and raised in the area, taking the mountains and the beach and the city itself for granted in a way an outsider never could. Ally could see that. It was obvious she knew what it felt like to belong to a place.

The longer we were out on that roof, the more we talked with that liveliness that comes when you meet someone special; someone who not only sees the world, but knows the world in a way that resonates with you. Our eyes were bright with whiskey and shyness and excitement; our glasses sat empty, forgotten on the ledge. The more time went on, the more I didn't want whatever this was to end. I spent my weekends on the mountain, ripping down cliffs on my board or climbing the highest peaks I could find. This moment, right here, felt something like that.

"So," Ally turned to me from where she was leaning, filling the pause in conversation, mischief all over her face, "What next?"

What next. Those two words would change me.

***

The next thing I knew we were flying down the highway toward the coast in the semi-comfort of my old Landcruiser, each bump in the road bouncing us in our seats in time to the music Ally had connected to the crackly stereo. Her smile was huge and her eyes were closed, head back against the seat and the wind from the open windows whipping her hair and it was like she was filling the entirety of the passenger side of the car. I couldn't wipe the slight smile from my face, the breeze winding itself through my dark curls and making the hair on my tanned arms stand every so slightly. At least, I think it was the wind giving me chills.

"What?"

I was startled out of my trance, the road and the music and the company.

"What?" Ally repeated, giggling. She was looking at me with her full attention, foot tapping along slightly to the guitars and the drums and the voices.

I tended to listen more than talk, observe rather than contribute.

"Nothing," I smiled back, an easy sort of smile, a slow smile, to compliment her fast and scattered. "I just like this."

My attraction to her, to this time and place, wasn't necessarily romantic. We'd just met, after all. It was more like life itself had shoved itself in my face, with all its thrills and journeys and possibilities, begging me to participate in a way I'd never considered.

We pulled out onto a cliff overlooking the ocean just as the last of the light slipped below the horizon. I'd been here a million times before, sometimes with friends and a 6 pack of beer, sometimes with girls that wanted more and sometimes they got it. This was different, though. I was seeing this view for the first time, living it through the awed "this is gorgeous" and "I can't believe this is our world" flowing from Ally beside me. We soaked in the sea salt air, the feeling of being nothing in comparison to what stood before us, stars beginning to appear in the midnight blue sections of sky.

We grabbed cheap beers and fresh fish and chips from the lone plank-clattered building we saw lit up a ways from where we stood on the cliff. Ally made small talk with the man taking our order while we waited for our food, breaking his crusty weathered face into something resembling a smile when she waved and shouted goodbye to him on our way out the door. I was in charge with making sure our food got safely back to the car; Ally couldn't be trusted with fries.

The salt left on our lips was indistinguishable from the salt on our freshly-dipped bodies. We huddled, shivering, in blankets borrowed from the build-out in the rear of my SUV, exchanging quiet thoughts and hopes and dreams.

"Sam? What do you think of when you look at the

sky? What do feel when you run into the ocean?"

I don't know why it was so simple sharing the most complicated parts of me with a stranger. Maybe because Ally didn't feel that way. She was a mystery, yes. But she was also home, a place I wanted to be.

***

I rolled over as the clock beeped 7am, groaning and squinting at the red numbers filling my vision. Images from adventures with a wild-haired girl filled my mind. It felt like a dream.

A scroll through my phone, blurry images of highway and ocean and stars filling my recent photos. Then, there — frizzy hair and whiskey and the biggest smile you could imagine, a rush of trees framed in the window behind her. She was real. Yesterday was real.

Our night had been cut short with Ally rushing to the airport, catching a flight to her next destination, onto the next adventure. I didn't want her to go, her light was contagious, brightening up life in a way made me feel her cold departure as soon as she hugged me goodbye and dashed out of the car into the night.

"It was so good to meet you, Sam," she had said.

Cliché, generic. The opposite of our night.

"Thanks for showing me a piece of you. I think it's rare, this connection we have. Did you feel it?"

Did I ever.

I looked out at the morning fog, the wet trees and rushing traffic, Thursday's jeans a dark huddle on the floor. There was an emptiness in me that could only be explained by a lack of Ally by my side, a reminder of her ability to not only fully immerse herself in the moment, but to allow others to rest there as well.

"What next?" she'd asked.

I would echo these words to myself for years to come, picturing her smile every time.

Space Simmer

Lauren McMahon

The afternoon sun glistened upon the peaceful water that swallowed up the yellow pit of sand, which was heavily peppered with inner-city holiday makers enjoying what was left of Summer holidays. Ah, just the way Lucy liked it. No waves meant no possibility of getting stuck in a rip the way her brother had recently, striking back hard against the shifty turbulence, forty degree wind pushing against his face.

"Hurry up Luce, last one in the water pays for hot chips!" Lucy rolled her eyes as Jake dropped his gear, skipped across the shallow water and dove headfirst into the drink. He was that always excited, always high on life kind of guy. those ones whose heart beat an extra beat, who would be at your door at 8 am every morning of the school holidays and wouldn't leave until he'd eaten his weight's worth in sausage sandwiches. It was as though his heart beat extra, spurring him on, leaving him breathless and hungry.

The cool water washed Lucy's skin clean of sweat and sunscreen. Finally, some relief from the melting heat. She floated on her back, exposing her navy swimsuit to the sun drowned crowd of leathery skinned city folk. . Nature was Lucy's best friend, other than Jake of course. Nature was always there for her to enjoy, nature never gave up, never left, unlike her father who'd walked out when Lucy was nine years old, leaving her, Ryan and Mum to take care of the family butcher's shop.

Floating here alone, Jake's yells and splashes barely registered. The white clouds moved apart and back together, sharing a loose rhythm she tried to imitate with her limbs. Reaching, pulling, weaving. For a moment, they parted, a second sun appearing in their wake. Lucy squinted, tried to blink the black circle from her retina.

"You know Lucy, if you do decide to turn vegan, despite all advice to the contrary, I might have to give you up as a friend. The hypocrisy just kills me: the butcher's vegan daughter."

She smiles. He loved threatening to lose her as a friend. But there, at the edge of her vision, the glowing outline of something indeterminate still hung in the wide-open sky. Something she had seen before. For a second she felt like maybe she had been singing the edge of something forever, something she couldn't quite grasp.

"Jake," Lucy said. "Have you ever felt like all your life you were simply connecting dots in a myopic puzzle designed by something entirely outside of your control?"

The waves lulled around them. His silence sank into the sea.

***

The next morning, Lucy woke to Jake banging relentlessly on her bedroom window. "Wake up Luce, I'm starving!" It was 9am on Saturday morning and Lucy's bedroom temperature gauge already read 29 degrees. She wiped her forehead and a glimmering line of sweat appeared against her forearm.

Jake pulled two bowls from the kitchen, placed two Weetbix in each and poured the white milk around them like a pool. It had become apparent to Lucy that over the last twelve months or so, her mum had started treating Jake like her own child. She would feed him, kiss his forehead, make him do chores, even yell at him if necessary. Jake essentially lived with them. He hated going home to his virtually empty house with only his dad occupying the lounge room, cans of Jack Daniels lined up at his feet. It was a sad reality and one that Lucy's mum seemed to know too much about.

A distant voice floated into the kitchen, interrupting their plans.

"Lawn please you two," mum said.

It took approximately two hours to mow the front lawn. The old Victa mower needed a new blade and spat out chunks of grass every couple of metres. Once Lucy and Jake had finished, they were greeted with a glass of ice-cold Cottee's cordial, rounds of condensation clinging to the outside of the glass and dripping down their necks. They hung their heads back in the plastic chairs on the concrete garden path, pointing out figurines in their dance across the opaque sky. As one cloud moved out of view, Lucy immediately began to sweat at the sight of the same orb, the same planet-like globe, hanging in the sky above their suburban home like a golden disk.

***

"Now to some breaking news this evening. Scientists are baffled as satellite images show Venus is moving closer to planet earth. Gerard Humphrey joins us now. Gerard, what can you tell us about the situation, and should viewers be alarmed?"

"Well Sandra, after joining our nation's scientists here at the Australian Space Agency it's clear that this is a once-in-a-million-year astronomical event. What we have been able to identify is that this is the planet Venus, as you've said, and it has moved close enough to be visible in our sky. It is likely she will remain in our view for – perhaps – months before resuming her usual trajectory, so try and enjoy her presence."

Lucy slumped into the carpet. She watched as Jake's eyes followed the reporter's as she consulted a giant 3D map of earth's atmosphere, the moon, and the relation of Venus to terra firma. She squeezed her eyes shut. She did not have to look at the orange-hued sky or the glistening map to know what was coming.

The hairs on her arms fizzed and smoked. Like standing too close to a fire. She breathed the ashy living room air. Not again, she whispered into her arms. She remembered the last time, the tremble of the earth's core pushing up against her body, the bubbling feeling in her blood. The way her chest ridged and seemed to split apart as the earth crumbled around their home. And now Venus was here. More potent than simple tectonic shudders.

The reporter was speaking again.

"Is it just me or has it felt hotter the last couple of days?" Mum pondered in between her sips of evening coffee.

***

By 5am the sky had opened again, the red orb giant in the sky, the moon fading slowly – creamy pink in Venus' reflective light. On the street, something was happening. Lucy's neighbour, an older Italian gentleman who ran the local pizza shop with his wife, was yelling hysterically, "Greta! Greta!" Lucy peered from her window, staring at Greta who was walking slowly down her driveaway, eyes glued to Venus, trance-like and strange. At the nature strip, Greta removed her shoes and dug her toes deeply into the grass until her nails pierced the dirt.

The whole street seemed to be looking on as the communion between woman and planet took place. Greta, normally inanimate, looked rapt: skin translucent, arms loose at her sides. She let out an ecstatic cry. Slowly, as if mimicking her own dreams, Lucy watched as flames seemed to erode her mortal body from the inside. Greta's skin moved, lifted, and finally fell in an ash-grey heap against the dirt and grass. Lucy's chest heaved. She pinched herself so hard that she bled.

On the street: the husband's strangled cry.

Within minutes the whole street was filled with emergency vehicles, their lights flashing so bright the morning sky couldn't be seen. "She had been feeling sick in the stomach, she thought she ate some bad fish, now she's gone! Her skin fell to pieces, what is this disease?" Greta's husband sobbed to the police, who appeared to be very suspicious of him.

***

Scientists had coined the term 'space simmer'. An unexplainable event within the human body that would cause core temperatures to spike, boiling the blood and causing the body to burn from inside out. Around the world, people began to show symptoms of high fever, nausea, dizziness and delirium. Some seemed to fight the power within their veins, while others would wake in the early hours of the morning, stand in full view of Venus before disintegrating into ash-like pieces, cooking in the planet's pungent heat.

The world went into lockdown. No one was to leave their homes; people were too terrified stand outside in view of Venus. All air travel ceased, schools closed down and men in special suits would drop food at doors. And still each night, more disappeared, wandering through the streets to open fields, nothing but steam and heat and baffled scientists in their wake.

***

Each day, the temperature rose. Lucy, Mum, Ryan and Jake tried to keep cool with cold showers and cups of iced water. The heat from the their bodies was now enough to singe cloth. Jake fussed with iced towels, wrapping Lucy's head and arms, sitting and watching as she grew calmer and warmer with every passing minute. Mum and her ate frozen meat from the butcher freezers. They spent weeks playing card games, hidden away from the outside world, curtains shut, and doors locked.

"I wish we could go for a surf!" Jake whined.

Lucy felt sick at night. Hot and bothered, she would rinse herself off in a cold shower, only to sweat again as soon as she was out. She had vomited twice after pretending all day that she was fine. Once everyone had succumbed to heat stroke, she would find herself dizzy besides the toilet. Some days Lucy felt scared and some days, when she thought of her favourite times spent floating on the ocean, glaring into the sky above, she felt at peace with the world, with nature, with what Earth had to do in order to survive.

She thought of all the interesting things she learnt in science the year before, the levels of crust beneath her, the oxygen that trees release so that she can breathe, the gravity that kept her stuck to the planet, the space beyond the ozone layer that was always a mystery to her. She thought of how the world had changed, how many of nature's cycles have been destroyed by humans, the air pollution, the animal distinction, the greenhouse gases causing the earth to heat up. Perhaps, Lucy thought, this is nature trying to fix what humans have broken. Eliminating us one by one.

One morning, Lucy rose suddenly to her feet, walked past Ryan's bedroom, then Mum's and finally past the lounge room where Jake was sleeping. She unlocked the back door, peered up at the sky where moon shone brightly beside Venus' harsh red surface. It was still dark, and she could faintly hear the sea crashing on the shore near her house. She walked to the rhythm of the waves, finding a lump of dirt to dig her toes in, face towards the sky above her.

"Luce! What are you doing? Get inside! Lucy!" Jake called from the back door, but she did not hear him. Only the crashing of waves and the buzzing of insects below filled her ears. Her stomach burned, but she did not resist the fire that consumed her for she knew that this was nature's way. Her skin turned to ash. First her arms, then her chest, her stomach, her head and then finally her legs.

"No! No! Lucy!" Jake screamed, as he watched his best friend being soaked into the dirt, disappearing before his eyes.

The World Turns

Linda Edorsson

Last time she saw Charity was a crisp Monday morning. She had wispy long hair ensnared by a messy braid resembling a withered hemp rope and a faded fluorescent scarf wrapped around her dirty neck. She was once beautiful but the streets had worn her thin as if she was a shell about to evaporate into dust.

A couple of coins made a rattling sound at the bottom of Charity's paper cup as she shook it in embarrassment, trying to preserve her energy for a long day of observing culotte hemlines. "Here," Sadie said to Charity, handing her a scalding long black, "have a lovely rest of your day." She quickly put it down on the ground. Sadie's ponytail was already bopping down the street in a hurry. Charity formed her lips to a, "Thank you," but swallowed the words into an empty stomach, sucked her burned thumb, and wiped it on her stockings. She had seen better days.

This was their weekday routine; a cup of warmth for an eased conscience. Nevertheless, Sadie noticed when Charity was gone that morning - or had she been gone the day before as well? She'd like to think she was the kind of person who would have noticed straight away but come to think of it she knew nothing about this woman on the street corner outside Meyer's. They had shared a smile or two and an occasional word but that was it. The story on the news was that they had all just vanished; the world was scraped clean of society's outcasts, leaving people in confused shrugs and echoing mumbles. Nobody knew what to do about it so they closed their curtains a little earlier, and held on to their belongings as if any of that would save them. The hummed whispers grew as rumours spread that a second rapture was coming, that governments were hiding secrets - or that they simply got sick of the world and took off.

The inevitable fear nobody dared to speak of was this: once the bottom layer of society had gone, it had to be replaced.

People couldn't believe they would disappear completely. It had been such an absurd thought but the empty streets at night proclaimed reality had changed. They had always been there as a comforting cushion, ensuring the population they weren't doing quite as bad as them. People may not have said it or thought it but they were content in their daily lull. That was how the world turned. The fact that elimination came as a surprise meant everyone played their part well. Now nothing was standing between the people left and the edge of obliteration.

Sadie had checked the lock on her apartment door four times that night. It was locked every time but she couldn't shake this uneasy feeling that someone was watching her, wanting to break in. "This is ridiculous" she thought, "I just need to get out of my head and get some fresh air." The world was a mess but she would try her best to distract herself. On the top floor was a ladder leading to the roof. Sadie had climbed there many times; it was perfect for sunbaking in spring. This night she brought a thick blanket to keep warm. A full moon reflected on the sides of the rooftop vents. She made sure she could get back to the stairwell by tucking her beanie in between the lock and the hatch. The sharp shadows cast from the chimneys creped her out. "Just a couple of deep breaths and then I'll hurry back to my warm bed." Her nose tingled as she let the night fill her lungs. A gust of wind made her hair flicker.

Bang!

Sadie spun around; the warm light from the stairwell was gone. She rushed to the hatch as if getting there faster would allow her to open it. A glimmer blinded her for a second and she fell as something sharp pierced her leg. Her stomach turned as she looked down to see gently pulsating dark lava. Blood leaked quickly from the wound to form a warm delta.. She felt like cold hands were holding her throat. Trying to swallow almost made her vomit. The door still locked against her weight.

Would she survive on the roof long enough for anyone to come looking for her? She wondered if her cubicle would be as loud as the empty street corners without her on Monday. Would anybody care if she didn't turn up at work? She started to feel hollow. Shivering, she applied as much pressure as she could to the wound. She thought she could outline a dark figure moving by the rooftop vent. Was this how the misfits had evaporated into thin air? Secret assassins hiding in dark corners ready to take you out when the world no longer needed you or stopped noticing? A clicking noise grew louder in her head, like steps moving closer. Sadie turned around, heart dropped, but as her eyes focused, all she could see were two threatening chimneys standing guard. Warm breath whispered in her ear, "Here."

She knew that voice, and her veins froze as she

swallowed a gulp from Charity's bitter long black. It burned her throat. "Did you only have confidence in your step because you were crushing people as you walked?" Charity's hazel eyes stared accusingly into Sadie's. With confusion, Sadie stuttered "No, I never walked on anyone." She felt annoyed more quickly than she wanted to admit and she twisted and pulled out a shard of metal, shaped like a knife, from her leg. Sadie could see Charity's reflection in the bloodstained shard. It looked twisted. There was something ominous about Charity's voice as she said, "We all learned how to walk but you were never afraid to fall," she continued as if she was an angel of doom. "Well I just fell, are you happy now?" Sadie grunted. "There were always people there to catch you." Charity murmured. "I don't see anyone coming to help me, is this about revenge?" Sadie asked breathlessly. Charity walked calmly towards the edge of the roof, her braid swayed in the cold night air. "Wait!" Sadie pleaded, "You can't leave me here." Sadie rushed to her feet, vertigo made the stars spin as she stumbled towards the figure moving closer to the edge. She threw herself after the worn down coat. Grabbing hold of a shoulder, she tumbled to the ground.

"I'm trapped." Sadie cried. "Are you?" Charity said laughingly. "I'll tell you what trapped feels like: the skin starts popping and turn liquid before the flames even hit you. But people don't want to hear that it hurts; they want to believe that numbness kicks in before pain, but it doesn't."

"Disappearing?" Sadie wondered.

"Is that what you call it?" Charity replied. "It feels like worms wiggling around just under your skin, but you can't kill them and make them stop without ripping your own flesh open. Ice cold - but that's just a trick of the mind - blisters forming telling of unbearable temperature. The hue of the skin changing, rolling over, like a swelling wave, from ivory to charcoal, slowly eating porcelain, as if it were cereal turning soggy in a deep bowl of milk. It slips off your bone and the smell burns hotter than the heat. Pain fills your senses. There is no silver lining."

"I didn't know." Sadie defended herself.

"You mean you didn't want to know." Charity's words bit through the air.

It had been easy to belong to the middle in a world created to fear the brim.

Sadie had heard enough. She held Charity out in the cold until she whimpered and fell silent. It burned her hands. In that moment it was as though her mind was filled with fire singeing her ears and whispering, "Do it". She could feel it eating her brain and turning her heart to concrete. "You're next if you don't." There was no one but Sadie on the roof, no more whispering ghosts. She had shut her up.

Sadie threw the bloody shard over the edge of the roof with shivering hands. Sadie slowly opened her eyes as they welled up with tears.

"This is the way the world turns."

Carrion

Charlotte O'Neill

One

You could not speak English when we met. I mean, you barely spoke at all. But between the grunts and gurgles, you rambled in French like a petit oiseau. Your eyes were moody storm eyes. Above them grew eyebrow hair, dark even then, meeting above your lashes in the middle in a thin line that you pushed together further in frowns. You were the most frustrated child and could force such terrible quiet when you worked. Nobody disturbed you, face bent close to small objects, placing the wings of dragonflies onto glue-ended sticks, bottling up a legless lizard in methylated spirits. Clear canopic jars with mice, grenouilles. You would drag me into your room and point at them, name them in quick French. I learned the words because at that point, you refused to learn mine. Your room was clean. Wood floors, a wide bed, a chest of drawers with neatly folded clothing placed inside their cavities, and a taxidermy eagle in the corner with bright glass eyes that hovered over everything.

Outside, a long hill ran down from the house into tangled bush. Described by real estate magazines as 'sub-tropical', the area was an elysian countryside that bridged sandy ocean dunes and green farmland. There your parents grew a failing olive farm, devoted to the oily fruits, with large presses that squeezed the fat from them into sweet virgin oil that your mother and you sold at local markets and boutique restaurants where lines of liquor stood behind bulbous chili plants in painted buckets. Nearby to the house lay a pool shaped like a giant marrow, filled with water and lined with painted stones as though the earth had birthed it. Your mother threatened to whip you if she caught you pissing in la piscine, at which we laughed, and you looked like you would swallow her if you could only grow large enough. Jon was seldom at home, but his fingerprints were left on everything as though lycopodium had been sprinkled across all the surfaces of the home, revealing his touch, and the white powdering spores where he had not touched.

As a very small child you failed to crawl. You slid along the ground like a serpent, dragging yourself by your forearms and moving in a squiggling line along the tiled kitchen floor. Then, suddenly one day, you pulled yourself up by the keys of a piano with a loud cacophonic burst that echoed throughout the house, stood and held yourself until somebody saw you. I was not there when this happened, it is a story your mother told me later, must have told me four or five times. I think she wondered if you not crawling had caused a missed beat. She always spoke of it as though it was something you forgot to do in the urge to walk.

In the evenings, your mother bar-tended at the local pub. She wore casual tee shirts and ripped black denim shorts, smudged her eyes with black liner and I wanted to be just like her. To get there from your house was fifteen minutes of winding sandy-sided backroads, shrubs and ferns sticking up at the bases of tall gums and cedars. The whole thing a motley dull green until the rains came and left paddocks sparkling viridescent. Sometimes she took you to the pub and you scavenged in the yard out the back, fossicking for bones or echidna needles and occasionally coming across a snake. If you found a snake you could sit for minutes totally still, while it slithered around you.

I don't know who told you that if a person were to be entirely motionless that a biting thing would not hurt them, but there you were sitting in the piece of land between the beer garden and somebody's cattle farm looking defiantly at a wriggling brown snake when I first saw you. I muffled a yell against the arm of my coat and without looking at me you raised a hand for quiet. I stood transfixed as you slowly stood up and backed away from it, and said to me in a voice that I haven't yet been able to decide is plaintive or defiant, it isn't going to hurt anyone.

I wandered back inside, took a seat with my family and watched as the night air wrapped itself like fog around my father's yellow beer. He pulled it to his lips and each time he plonked it back onto the table the fog crystallised, dripped, and I counted the concentric circles made on the wood that blurred into one another. At the back of the pub my uncle played a twelve-string guitar and sang, and his beard touched the strings. The fingers on his right hand were long with grown out nails that leapt and wound the crowd up until they swayed and bobbed, moved to the beat or closed their eyes and waited until his voice possessed them. His face tightened and relaxed with each sentence as he sang them and at the end he yelled out into the crowd for my father to join him and they played together, dad on a harmonica that he pulled from his pocket and uncle banging his proper leg up and down, the guitar a living thing and his fingers reptilian in their cool temper.

One such night, six years later, you followed the drunken car as it swayed through fog and by-passed cattle, but in the morning, I awoke and you were gone.

Two

Louise floated through the house and surprised us many times as I sat on the floor, you lying on your stomach. You accused her of sneaking around. I must have met your father once or twice when we were that young. On brief returns from overseas, many times drunk, often angry or ecstatic, never sombre. It was strange, when I returned as an adult, to find him both sober and silent, and your mother with a voice loud enough to echo through the house from one end to the other.

It did not seem odd to me then, but it does now, that I was so often at your house. It was not the sort of thing that as a child I considered. We (my brother, sister, and I) were simply taken, and left there, and then mother (who you called Mim or Mimi and whose name was Miranda) would return from town or pilates or hot yoga and collect us. When you were eight and I was twelve we snuck into the kitchen late one evening when the parents were in the front yard by the pool hosting a barbeque, and we found Louise's phone book. It must have been about ten in the evening, so we prank called everybody. You spoke to them in French and became more and more frustrated when they would not respond to your very insistent questions. Eventually this game was not fun anymore and we went to your room which was always dry and woody and dancing with the chromatic lights used for your snake tank, but in the morning Louise found out about the phone book and told your father, who gave you a broken lip and asked you if you would like to find yourself at the bottom of the pool one day.

I imagined drawing your body from the blue crystalline pool, parting your lips with one hand.

Three

The area our parents lived was made up of coastal farms. From the sky, when catching a flight in, it looks like a grid. Rectangles lie next to each other, like a piece of camo material laid out on the ground. There are patches of brown, tan, green and very dark green like the moss that grows in a fringe around the trunks of trees. The further from the coast one drives, the darker the colours, and the more insistent the smell of rotting leaves and wet mud. By the sea the beach is white, with tiny shells that feel like coarse sand underfoot. Occasionally, surfers dart in and out. The water lurches at walkers. It is deceptively calm on cool days, and on a windy day looks wild with whiteness. After a storm, foam is pushed in from far at sea to create a swirling mess of dirty froth that dances like a blizzard on the sand.

I remember we were walking along the beach, picking at shells. We wanted to create a cardboard dragon out of old boxes and then glue shells of different sizes all over its skin to create the illusion of a bumpy, rigid surface. Skin worn hard. We were taking the shells and putting them into a bag that Louise had given us, a bag made of fabric with an abstract tree with fruits on it that made it look as though the bag had water droplets on it. We must have lost track of the time. The colours were almost feral in the sky; drunk purple hues that chased the small white clouds away. The air became filled with a turgid energy and we began to run, pushing each other and playing and moving closer and closer towards the edge of the sea where some of the white blizzard froth had built up.

Soon you were running through it, carving a deep path that filled behind you immediately with salty water and suds. You ran blithely and your feet seemed to be pulled at odd angles, deep parts of the sand sucking at you. And then you fell into the foam. I couldn't see you and I looked around for somebody to tell, and then rain towards where it seemed you had disappeared. I ran in circles in the frothy sea, worrying about what I had been told about toxin run-off building up in sea foam and travelling in to shore just like this. It felt like a long time that I tried to look for you, but it mustn't have been long, and eventually I just stood and looked around, hoping to see an arm move or the foam shift like a boy's body might. And then I felt my back being hit by something hard, and I was in the foam too, and you were laughing and taunting me and calling me a loser, and I fought you in the foam until you panted and said arrêtez, arrêtez. And we did not make the shell-encrusted dragon, but rather returned home and ate Louise's olive paste on white sourdough bread drizzled with oil and drank hot chocolates by the fire, and this night nobody threatened either of us.

Four

It is 6:30am and I had snuck out of the house to see you.

Hand in hand we walked across fields, my pants dewy and heavy from the water held by the grass in the morning fog. You in a flannel shirt and a long pair of black jeans, a pair of work boots. You talk about the trees, the names of them, you lose the grip of my hand to skirt the area for snakes or venomous spiders, for a blue tongue lizard to hold and show me.

Everything seems to come alive for you.

You stop me, pull me onto the ground, force me to look at the green belly of a chrysalis growing on a milkweed, and you tell me it is a monarch chrysalis, common, and to look over there - a monarch caterpillar. And I lay back into you, wondering. And your arms are dendrous, as you mark my body. You move between my limbs with the sober insistence of the wind. Your gold hair falls between my fingers and you tell me things that I am not sure I really care about.

The morning doesn't pass, it moves around us like the sun moves around the earth.

You unearth me. Draw my roots up from the ground. Leave me lying against the soft grassy earth in all its damp viridity. Our bodies mark the ground and I have never left this place, not once.

Five

Louise met your father in France. In the eighties. When they met she was wearing a bright pink checked suit, and sneakers, and her hair was permed and half-tied at the top of her head. He said, she was the least French looking girl I'd seen in my life. She went to France after America, quitting her first year of a business degree and leaving her family in Australia to travel. They met when she had almost run out of money, and walking from restaurant to restaurant in Strasbourg, along the Rue du Fosse-des-Tanneurs to the water where restaurants and nightlife shimmer. Looking like a tourist, she had walked into the restaurant that he owned at the time - him, sitting at a table near the kitchen, scribbling lists of bills and sipping a black coffee. She asked at the till if they needed somebody to wait, and they said maybe, and to ask the owner. The way he tells it, that was it. She stayed in France, moved into his apartment, and did not come back until she became pregnant and went absolutely fucking ballistic.

I used to think about this a lot. Wondering, what made a person go crazy. And then, when your father began to call you crazy too, I doubted that your mother had been.

By the light of the lunatic moon your face arrives with me, night by night. A steady treasure. Golden, my tears cover your skin.

Six

There is a creek that falls through the paddock.
Rocks lie dormant in its path. Ticks hide in the grass.
The arboreous skyline moves slowly. Above the creek
are trees too, long branches meeting over the water,
dropping leaves that clutter the surface and are pushed
away, creating false edges beyond the bank. On the
rocks lizards bake and so do we. We hear the trickle of
the stream, and it merges with the sounds that in
normal, conversation-filled circumstances would blur
away totally from focus. The sounds of things slipping
through dry grass, occasional moos from cows too far
away to see, and the buzzing sound of wings. Some of
them are visible to us. A blue dragonfly melts onto a
rock flowing with water, legs submerged, long tongue
drinking deeply.

Every now and again we reach a hand over and
dangle it in the cold to cool ourselves. The smell of
sweat is clear and salty, almost seems visible, like it isn't
so much evaporating off us as forming a cloud around
our bodies. It's heavy. Every few minutes a gust of wind
rushes up the gully. Hairs stand up all over my body. I
am suddenly aware of the hair at the back of my legs,
under the soft parts of my arms, on the sides of my
face.

We lie here for hours and take breaks from lying
by standing up and stretching or wandering upstream a
little and returning back. After a while you get bored
and you take off. I lose sight of you quickly, as the banks
are steep and covered in long grass and trees. You
don't look back.

With you gone, the gully feels like a chasm and the wind seems to bite. There is none of the camaraderie of sticking it out, getting cold and hot again. I don't realise it at the time but I like this place because I like to watch you, and now that you've run off, I get bored quickly. Sitting alone, I flick pieces of dirt into the creek and watch them sink. A shadow falls over my skin and I shudder and move up the grassy embankment. The sun is heavier there, and I stretch out at an awkward angle. Despite, or because of, the sudden aloneness, I fall asleep.

When I wake up, you're still not back, and I wait until the sky turns orange for you but you've gone.

Seven

It should've occurred to me at the time, how often you did this, but it didn't. You'd just disappear. Maybe it taught me a lot of things about abandonment. Maybe I wanted to abandon you one day. Who knows. But I didn't like it.

I arrived home that evening frustrated at myself. I snapped at my father at dinner when he made jokes and touched my cheek. Mum asked how the day had been. Great, says her sullen child. You're sunburnt. Make sure you get some aloe vera on those cheeks.

I wandered around outside for a while and when I came back in, she'd placed two open pieces of aloe vera plant on a plate. Their stringy, wet insides were leaking. I took one then the other and rubbed the cool vaporous membranes across my burnt skin. It smelled like water and armpits and cucumber.

Eight

All this time, I have been writing to you as though you were gone. What will I do when I can see, or imagine seeing, you really? When you are not the same as your ghost. How do I find you? What if I come where you are? These are questions I only ask of myself when I am here, laying on the cool sand on a grey evening, or drifting alone down a grass lined dirt road, hearing the euphonic evening sounds emerge. At university these questions are sucked out of me. I enquire, categorise, obtain, evaluate, attempt to surpass myself, barely pass myself. And it is very difficult to think out there, on the barren steps of buildings filled with words.

The Writers

Amity Bradford is a English major education student at Avondale University College. Her corona survival kit includes: marshmallows, wool and a quality read from Ondaatje.

Sally-Mae Herford is an English and Visual Arts student teacher at Avondale University College. She loves singing in the car, vanilla oat cappaccinos, watching movies with twist endings and then ruining said movie ending to any of her friends that will listen to her for more than five minutes.

Linda Edorsson is a freelance writer, filmmaker and a communications graduate from Avondale University College. She's ardent about storytelling with a soft spot for the weird ones. She enjoys people watching over coffee, exploring the outdoors for hikes and going ice-skating on the lakes of Sweden where she's from.

Lauren McMahon is an English literature student at Avondale University College. She is passionate about supporting young people in their navigation of social issues and solutions. She loves a Winter's bonfire surrounded by family and friends, roasting marshmallows and singing songs.

Calum Entermann is an aspiring English Teacher who likes to read and run but not all at once. He is thrilled to be alive in the time of spell-check and to know that his to-read list will never run dry.

Kathryn Staples is an English and History student at Avondale University College. She enjoys sitting by the fire enjoying a nice hot tea and a piece of cake while listening to music to relax and unwind. Her passion is to bring a smile to everyone's face as much as she can.

Caitlin Jankiewicz is studying English and Mathematics Secondary Education at Avondale University College. When she's not buried in math homework she enjoys writing, baking and rock climbing. Nothing sounds better to her than an afternoon with a good book and a purring cat.

Lachlan Bilson is a Technologies and English teaching student at Avondale University College. He is an adamant advocate of the Aussie adventure experience, never missing an opportunity to tour the great outdoors and meet someone or experience something new. Some of his other passions include his family, folk music and his search for the Hunters best burger shop.

Ashley Cotter is an American living in Australia, because she has access to healthcare here. She barely graduated from Avondale with a double major in Marketing and Communications with a minor in Graphic Design (if it sounds like a lot, it was - don't do it). When she's not forgetting to press send on already written emails, she likes adventures and coffee to fuel them, and is often found getting distracted by anything and everything.

Lynnette Lounsbury is a writer, poet, wanderer and lecturer who lives in Sydney, Australia and who likes to follow the sun and loves a good zombie story. She has published two novels and is always writing another one.

Charlotte O'Neill is a contemporary Australian poet, writer and teacher from Byron Bay NSW. She writes on a variety of themes involving women's experience, cultural and social issues affecting the youth, grief, trauma and mental illness. Her debut poetry collection Then The Bones Blossomed is available through Vivid Publishing.

Acknowledgements

This book owes its existence to the encouragement of many people but in particular Carolyn Rickett for advice, encouragement and unwavering support and Jim Lounsbury for poetry and publication advice.

The cover of this book was designed by Donna Pinter, Design & Prosper Pty Ltd.